RIDING THE STORM
A Memoir of Mental Illness

RYAN HARLAND

RIDING THE STORM

ISBN: 9781074733742

Imprint: Independently published

This book was written with the
assistance of Your Memoir

For further information contact
Marnie Summerfield Smith

yourmemoir.co.uk

marnie@yourmemoir.co.uk

07710 721 389

Author photograph: James Hughes Photography

DEDICATION

To Mum, for all you've done for me.
And for my girls, with all my love, always.

CONTENTS

ACKNOWLEDGMENTS

Thank you, Mum, for your unconditional love, for your unending support and for your loving care of Kevin and I.

Thank you, Marnie. I would not have been able to do this without you.

AUTHOR'S NOTE

THERE are people who don't want me to write this book. But I don't care. It's my story and I'm telling it.

I'm telling it because some of the events depicted have made me the man I am today. I'm telling it because it's about my ups and downs, and how I got through the trials and tribulations that life throws at us all. I'm telling it because I don't want to hide in the shadows anymore.

I will not feel ashamed because of my illness, or because of what I have experienced.

And this is my experience – my experience of living with Emotional Intensity Disorder (EID), so it will be different to yours. Every experience, and certainly the experience of mental illness, is subjective. I am speaking only for myself.

Having said that, I do want to take

responsibility and I want to apologise to anyone who has had to withstand the worst of my illness and me.

I've made mistakes. I've jumped from one relationship to another without considering other people's feelings. But I feel it is important that people understand why I am the way I am.

I do not choose to be like this. I would never choose to be like this. Would you?

I have now completed both the STEPPS and Stairways programs of group therapy specifically for people with EID. Getting onto these courses was a battle. In fact, getting any mental health assistance in the UK at this time is a battle, the horror of which disgusts me.

Are things changing? I don't know. Mental health is being talked about these days, but until more money is allocated, or it is better spent, there will not be enough staff to offer treatment – and offer it quickly, when people need it, not in two years' time. You don't have to wait two years to have your broken leg put in plaster, do you? I do not want to give any government the benefit of the doubt when people are suffering, and taking their own lives, and families are being impacted.

This book contains memories of sexual abuse, suicide attempts, self-harm and severe mental illness. If you feel it may trigger painful memories for you, please do not read it without support, or at all, until the time is right for you.

You will find information about mental health organisations at the back of the book. I encourage you to keep knocking on doors until you get the help you need. It's hard to advocate for yourself but I am rooting for you. You deserve to feel better. I am living proof that there is hope.

Ryan Harland,
Sheerness,
Isle of Sheppey,
Kent.
Summer, 2019

INTRODUCTION

IMAGINE you are wearing sunglasses. You are always wearing sunglasses. You never take them off.

Imagine you have 10 pairs and are always wearing at least one pair, maybe more, maybe all of them. You'd have to have a long nose and interesting-shaped ears. But that would be the least of your worries. Because these sunglasses are not there to protect you like normal sunglasses. They don't shield you from the sun and make you look cool and feel groovy. These sunglasses harm you. Each pair makes you see the world, and yourself, in a different way, a sinister, confusing, threatening way.

This is what it is like to have Emotional Intensity Disorder (EID) or Emotionally Unstable Personality Disorder (EUPD).

They used to call it Borderline Personality Disorder (BPD). The word borderline is misleading. It makes it sound as if this illness is between two things and not too bad, because you might have it and you might not.

But what borderline means in this context is that people with BPD are on the borderline between psychosis and neurosis.

Psychosis is a symptom that means people cannot distinguish what is happening within them from what is happening in the world. People in psychosis may have delusions and as a result, behave and communicate in an inappropriate or incoherent fashion. Neurosis is a symptom best described as anxiety and avoidance behavior.

Sounds complicated? Try living with it. Actually don't. But if you could try a little to understand it, that would help.

So back to the sunglasses. When you have EID, you view the world most of the time through one or more of these 10 pairs of very unhelpful sunglasses. In EID-world, these are called our filters. The filters are listed below. I have described how each one makes me feel and I have listed them 1-10 with one being the filter that can be the most intense for me and 10 being the one that affects me least.

1. Failure to Achieve: I am useless and will never achieve anything

2. Vulnerability to Harm and Illness: I will get sick and die

3. Subjugation: I must always do what others want, I am a people pleaser

4. Unrelenting Standards: I will never be good enough for anyone

5. Defectiveness/Social Undesirability: I will never belong. No one wants me in their group

6. Self-sacrifice: I must put others first at all time

7. Entitlement: I am entitled to anything

8. Abandonment: People have always and will always leave me

9. Emotional deprivation: I never get the love and care that I need

10. Mistrust: I can trust no one. I am on my own.

If you're still reading, well done. That list is bloody bleak, to be fair. And to be viewing every situation, every interaction with every other human, be it your Mum, your wife, your kids, your boss, your mates or someone on Facebook, through these filters is a horrendous way to live. Not surprisingly, this illness can shorten your life for many reasons. Including suicide.

So those are the filters, and in the STEPPS manual, a filter is described as "(an) extremely stable and enduring pattern of thinking that develops during childhood and is elaborated throughout an individual's like. We view the world through filters".

As a result of living with 10 pairs of the world's shittiest sunglasses, there are quite a few symptoms of EID.

You can Google all this stuff yourself but to give you an overview, the symptoms are emotional instability. I know! Who would have thought? Disturbed patterns of thinking, impulsive behavior and unstable relationships. Yup, yup, yup. I experience the full range of intense, negative emotions such as rage, sorrow, shame, panic, terror, emptiness and loneliness, sometimes on a daily, or even hourly, basis. I want people to leave and to stay at the same time. I view things as completely perfect or doomed. I am frightened. I am also a Sheppey season ticket holder, a Gillingham and Liverpool FC supporter, an indoor dancer, a lover of fish and chips and Chinese food and a fan of Friends, The Big Bang Theory, property programmes and The Undateables – a reality TV show that is so uplifting it should be on prescription.

I'm still me. And like I say, there is hope.

Here are a list of thoughts I recorded on my phone before I had targeted group therapy, the STEPPS program:

> I hate myself so much. I can't help being the way I am. I have demons inside that get me angry and confused about simple everyday tasks. I don't know how much of this flipping out I can take. I'm hurting so many people I love and my work colleges. I'm scared that one day it'll happen too much, that no one will want me in their lives and that I will be all alone.
>
> Sometimes I just want to shut myself away

from the world.

I'm a boy in a man's body, confused about what to do, and how to make myself happy. All I want is to be loved for who I am, to be accepted and to lead a simple but happy life. I'm not sure if it'll ever happen or it's even possible. Perhaps I have to face the fact that this is how my life is going to be.

I am trying so hard to concentrate and stay focused but it's getting harder every day. I can feel the whirlwind behind my eyes getting faster and faster and the pressure building up. I can't tell people how I truly feel as they have their own shit to deal with.

Would anyone notice if I wasn't here?

On the surface I may look like I'm keeping afloat with ease, but underneath the water, my legs are paddling frantically. I constantly feel too tired to continue so I take a break, then I start to sink and then I start to panic. That makes me sink even lower.

My head feels like a ticking time bomb. I feel the pressure building up and up which makes everything much harder to accomplish. I am waiting for it to explode.

I'd love to press the reset button and start again.

Here's one from afterwards:

I know I will always have my mental illness but I'm understanding it more and more every day. I am beginning to notice subtle changes in how I'm dealing with the situations that life throws my way and it's all good. The group I go to is helping a lot. I feel more positive about my future. I know I will still have bad days like everyone else but hopefully they won't be as frequent as they have been before. I sometimes wish I had a remote control and could rewind life and play it differently. But if I could do that, would I be the person I am today? I know that I am kind and compassionate and I'm glad about that. Everything I have been through has made me who I am.

So that's the sunglasses, for you. But for almost 40 years, I didn't even know I was wearing them.

CHAPTER 1

WHEN I was a little boy, I thought Smarties gave you magic powers. You remember Smarties, don't you? Different-coloured milk chocolates in crisp sugar shells rattling about in a tube. I haven't seen them about for ages. So many different types of chocolate and sweets these days.

But in the early 80s we didn't have too many choices. It didn't matter. Smarties were my go-to and they were cool.

I'd pop the little plastic lid off the end – there was always a different letter on the inside, educational purposes I suppose – and spill the coloured oblate spheroids (I had to look that up!) into the palm of my sweaty hand. Red, orange, yellow, lime green, lilac, pink and light brown. The blue ones replaced the brown ones in 1988 in a blaze of advertising glory; a stroke of marketing genius. Those old-school chocolates looked like magic pills and I knew that they would give me magic powers. Strength. That's what I thought Smarties gave me. Power and strength. I wish I believed that now. Because I'd eat as many as I could find.

Mum would buy me Smarties. She'd buy some for my older brother Kev too. He was four years my senior, born on December 15, 1973. We'd take them home and scoff them together. Sometimes we'd eat them in the den we'd made from blankets draped between the settee and the old wooden clothes dryer. Kev also believed Smarties gave him magic powers. He needed them. We all did.

I was born on July 11, 1977. My mother is Elizabeth. My father Michael Charles Harland, who I only ever refer to as SD – sperm donor. The four of us lived on the Isle of Sheppey in Kent.

Kev and I shared a room but when I was one, we moved and we got our own rooms. When I got a bit older I had bunk beds in my room, and Kev would sometimes come in and sleep in my room.

Both my parents are from the Isle of Sheppey. Mum's dad died years before I was born but I remember my mum's mum. She was tiny so Kev and I nicknamed her Little Nan. Mum visited her every day. They were really close. Kev and I always enjoyed visiting Little Nan, especially when SD was renovating our house and it was full of muck and dust. We went out so that he could get on with the work, but he never did.

At Little Nan's, Kev and I would play cards, usually Uno, and I would sneak into the cupboard and eat handfuls of her Kellogg's All-Bran. If I was tired, I would crawl under her sideboard and fall asleep. Not that I was a sleepy child. I was always 100 miles-an-hour. Little Nan and Mum always had each other's backs. Sometimes Mum stayed the night at Little Nan's when SD got too much for her.

I also spent a lot of time at my paternal grandparents' house. I called them Big Nan and Grandad. My Nan wasn't big, just big compared to my other Nan.

Every Sunday we would go there for tea. We'd have ham sandwiches with lots of mustard and jam, and cream sponge. Mum drove us there and SD was invited but often wouldn't come. It was one of a number of things that caused my parents' to have blazing rows. He would say he was at work but later be spotted walking through town. Anyone that questioned him got both barrels.

When we moved, SD worked at the local steelworks but took voluntary redundancy against Mum's wishes. He never really had a proper job afterwards. He did casual work, sometimes at exhibitions in London, but he never brought any money home. So Mum worked to make sure we got by.

But financial support wasn't the only thing lacking where SD was concerned. Often my Mum would wake up in the morning and find a strange bloke in the house, someone he had brought home. She can't believe she didn't twig what was going on, but she was very innocent, and SD terrorized her and was regularly violent.

When Mum was eight months pregnant with me, SD organized a street party for the Queen's Silver Jubilee. When she failed to bake any cakes for the event, he shoved her into a cupboard.

He would hit her round the head and use whatever he had in his hand at that moment as a weapon. He threw food at her, poured milk over her, threw our baby bottles at her, the remote control – it would all hit Mum or the wall and be smashed to pieces. He broke all the dinner plates once because she didn't help him to clear the snow. And there were times when he would abuse her in front of others. He threw a bottle of Coca Cola at her with his dad in the room, and once, when he was in hospital, he nearly swung at her in front of the doctor.

Violence towards women was more likely to be accepted back then, so no one offered my mother any support or an escape route. Domestic violence wasn't spoken about.

As well as verbally and physically abusing our mother, and emotionally abusing and terrorising the entire household, we discovered years down the line that SD sexually abused Kevin for 10 years, until my brother was 15.

Why are some people so cruel? Why are some destined to suffer at the hands of others? Why is there such evil in the world?

If only Smarties had the answer.

CHAPTER 2

"YOU can watch, Ryan, but don't touch," Kevin tells me. "I don't want you to break it."

My big brother's playing Lego. I watch, but heed his warning. He's dead serious. I adore him and want to be with him, so if I can look but not touch, that's fine by me. I enjoy watching him create things. I laugh when he concentrates because his tongue hangs out like a dog.

Kev likes to doodle too. We are arty children. We even wrote a book and sent it to Ladybird, hoping they would print it. We got a letter back saying: "Thank you for your story. Unfortunately, we're not going to do it this time." Kev did all the drawing and writing, actually. The letter was addressed Master Kevin and Master Ryan. Just to get that letter back from Ladybird was amazing to us.

We loved building camps by covering

furniture with sheets. On one occasion, a neighbour was having an extension built and there was a big pile of builders' sand out front. Kev and I were out there for hours constructing tunnels through which we would drive our Matchbox cars. They were happy memories. Happy times with Kevin, my mother, playing Lego, building camps, going The Strand in Gillingham, having a great time in the park by the river.

Kev and I argued, like brothers do, but we did do a lot together. He was very creative and made up stories and plays. He'd design costumes out of paper and paper clips for me to wear. I can remember walking around as a soldier once with all this paper wrapped round me.

Kevin was a quiet kid and very placid. He liked playing with his farmyard animals and enjoyed being indoors. Kind at heart, he once cared for our mother when she caught glandular fever and Bell's palsy. SD, of course, was completely devoid of sympathy for Mum while she suffered. Being an indoor child meant that Kev was far more exposed to the toxic environment created by SD.

Mum says she didn't know I was there for the first year I was born, but I made up for it after that. I was never still and it escalated when I was six or so, and I discovered football.

Even if it was in the back garden on my own, or on the drive or against a wall, again on my own, I was happiest with a ball at my feet. I was constantly shouted at for hitting windows and sending balls flying into the neighbour's garden. Football, football, football. If I wasn't at school, eating, or sleeping I played football wherever I could until I got called in at night, which would see me kick off because I wanted to stay outdoors and play. I had dreams of becoming a professional footballer. But didn't every boy?

One thing I had in common with the professionals – certainly those playing in the Premier League these days – was that I was very accident-prone. Unlike today's pros, though, I actually hurt myself. I once fell and hit my head on the curb. That hurt. Another time, I was playing football and smashed my eye socket on an iron gate. Gentler pursuits were just as dangerous. I cracked my head open playing cricket once. And even indoors I wasn't safe – I chipped my collarbone falling down Big Nan's stairs; I broke my arm crashing into a coffee table while jumping on a pouffe.

And despite burning up all this energy, Kev and I were both little buggers for going to sleep. So it was pretty hard on Mum.

My brother suffered from asthma and horrendous night terrors. Mum sat up with him night after night. She took him to the doctor, but no one guessed the real reason for Kev's nightmares.

When Mum found out that SD sexually abused Kev throughout his childhood, she beat herself up about it. But we never blamed her. Mum is the strongest woman I know. She's my best friend and I don't blame her for anything.

In fact, I thank her for the way she's brought me up. I've never blamed anything that's happened to me, or the way I am, on my Mum.

Despite how wonderful she was, parents can't always protect their kids. Not only was SD sexually abusing him, but Kevin was also bullied as a child. Kids said he looked like a monkey because of his prominent features. I don't know if that was the cause of him not going out much, but I shouldn't think it helped. To try to help him, we looked at joining a karate club, hoping it would boost his confidence. But he didn't want to take part. I took it up, though, and it was another activity that I could get my teeth into, so I was more than happy at the outset.

But it didn't last long. I got scared. It seemed as if there were two sides to me. I was very active, but I also wanted to be at home, indoors. Despite my eagerness to be playing football, cricket, anything, I was a timid child; I cried a lot. Every time Mum dropped us off at her mum's, I would chase after the car crying because Mum was leaving. I was very clingy, always emotional. I understand now that this is due to the intense fear of abandonment experienced by people with EID. My rational brain knows that, but my EID brain uses it as a stick with which to beat me.

CHAPTER 3

MUM was on tenterhooks. She would have spent all day tidying, cleaning and vacuuming but it was never good enough for SD. According to his unattainable standards, the place was a shithole and she needed to sort it.

"This place is a pigsty," he'd snap. "Sort it out."

"I had to know my place, or he would hit me," Mum recalls. "He was full of his own importance and if SD didn't get his own way there was hell to pay."

Mum questions why she married him. She was 27 and probably worried about being left on the shelf, she says, a real concern in those days. They married in September 1972.

SD no real interest in having children but since he only had one testicle he was obsessed with proving he was able to, Mum says. A year after they married, Kevin was born. It wasn't long before SD's frustration took its toll on Mum. Kevin had cried nearly all night long and as a result SD missed A train to London the following morning.

He yelled at Mum, demanding to know what was wrong with the baby. And then he hit her. That first time took her by surprise. And it just carried on. It became so bad she suffered a miscarriage due to one of his attacks.

Children pick up on a parents' fears, their anxieties. And we certainly absorbed all of it. Your home is supposed to be a place of safety. Our home was anything but. It was a frightening place, especially when SD was there. It was an unpredictable place; he was unpredictable. You never knew what he was going to do next.

I mostly recall him shouting constantly at Mum and on one occasion throwing and smashing plates. That must have been the time when he was furious that she hadn't helped him clear the snow. I'm sure I saw more than I remember. I always knew not to cross him. He scared me.

"Don't cross him, don't upset him, don't piss him off," was the message I received loud and clear.

We rarely went on holiday. SD did take us to Camber Sands once, but Mum describes it as horrendous. He left the caravan every night and she had no idea where he was going. He did the same thing during a family break in Hastings.

We later discovered that he was a Peeping

Tom and he would meet up with men. Even when Mum was pregnant with Kevin, SD would go out all night. She was never allowed to ask where he had been.

I know Mum feels now that she was very naïve, but she was under his control – and where she could have gone? Back then, there was little awareness of domestic violence, and virtually no support. Even now there's not enough.

SD's weird, creepy and obviously criminal behaviour caught up with him from time to time and the police would come to our house to talk to him.

One final night when SD didn't come home, Mum realized she'd finally reached the end of her tether. She phoned her mother-in-law, packed the car with our pillows, our three budgies in a cage and we left. It was June 15, 1989. I didn't understand why we were leaving; just didn't get it. I knew SD was an angry man but I felt guilty that he was now on his own. I was young, I suppose, just 11, Kev was 15, and we had nowhere to live, no money, no furniture.

Mum traipsed around Sheerness looking for somewhere we could live. First we stayed with her sister-in-law, then a friend's house. Then Mum's brother arranged for us to live in the house of someone he knew in Sheerness. That became home for four years. SD let us have our bunkbeds, which was big of him. He was court ordered to give Mum 5p maintenance a week for us boys. At the time a loaf of bread cost about a pound. She didn't accept it.

Despite the upheaval, this must have been a blessed release for Kev. I have only hazy memories of that time. The only thing I really remember is moving about. I just accepted it. I didn't know what was going on although I knew I was scared of SD. But now I was with Mum and Kev. And that's what mattered to me.

SD had barely had an input in my life, but I still felt obligated to go and see him. People might question my decision. I know I have. But the simple fact is that children are programmed to want their parents in their life and will revisit and revisit, hoping desperately things will get better, be different. Not only that, but I knew he'd kick off at Mum if I didn't go. He didn't want to see me, he just didn't want to lose face and admit to people that the three of us wanted nothing more to do with him, especially now that he was going to court and his crimes were being reported in the papers. There was a physical fight over custody of me that I remember. SD was pulling me with one arm, Mum with the other. But eventually she let go as she didn't want me to get injured. She called the police, but nothing was done.

So, I did the bare minimum. I'd pop over to SD's house before going out with my friends who lived nearby. He would ask me why Kev didn't come to visit. I told him I didn't know, which was true. They occasionally crossed paths at Big Nan's, but that was it.

Bubbling underneath was that sense that something bad had happened, or was going to happen. And sure enough, I started seeing and hearing more, reading stories about him in the paper.

We were watching the London Marathon on TV one Sunday, when there was a knock at the door. SD told me to get on the floor. We needed to hide because he owed someone money.

I wasn't always comfortable being in his house, being with him, but he would entice me with things like Sky TV – an 11-year-old football mad boy can be easily persuaded.

As I got older, I witnessed SD's temper more and more. Once, he was trying to get into our house. I had a big bottle of Coca Cola in my hand so I went up to the door and started hitting him in the head with it. I wasn't going to hurt him with plastic but I wanted him to leave. The neighbours gathered to watch me pummeling him, and he quickly changed his tune.

"Don't worry, Elizabeth, it's fine," he started to say. "We will get over this."

He was lying through his teeth as usual, putting on a mask for the neighbours, trying to make them think he was the victim, locked out of his house. He was a master manipulator.

It was always like that.

CHAPTER 4

ANYTIME I came home from visiting SD, I would have what Mum called, "the screaming abdabs". I was uncontrollable. I suppose I was scared of SD and when I got home, and felt safe, I could release all that fear.

They say you take it out on the ones you love and I was a fucking arsehole to Mum for years. We laugh about it now, but she called my alter-ego Fred. I was a completely different person and when I said sorry I would blame Fred. Maybe those were early signs of BPD, I don't know. I have worries that maybe SD had sexually abused me too and I've perhaps blocked it out. If that was the case, it might have been this that was causing me to flip out. I've thought about seeing a hypnotherapist, but do I want to know? Do I need to know? Even if I wasn't abused at a young age, I can see that I was traumatized in my younger years by the domestic abuse, the atmosphere of terror in our home. I was in a constant state of extreme vigilance and fear. I was afraid and powerless for so many years.

So Mum was on her own with me and Kev. She worked a part-time job but SD hung around outside and told her boss he didn't want the likes of Mum working there. Fortunately, Mum's boss didn't take any notice. Then, in the early 90s, Mum met Pete, who I regarded as my stepfather, and he lived with us for seven years until his death in 2000. I never classed him as a dad, but he was a better dad than SD was, even though we clashed big time.

SD's crimes, meanwhile, continued. At a party which SD was attending, a friend of mine passed out. While he was out cold, SD sexually assaulted him, during which my friend woke up. He beat SD up, and was jailed for two years. I'm still friends with that guy, and I've told him I wished he'd done a better job.

SD never went to prison for his misdemeanours. The most he got was a two-year suspended sentence. Every time the police would tell us he'd, "definitely go down this time". But he never did. There was always this sense of: What is he up to now? He was always in bother. Getting beaten up by my friend wasn't the first time he got a pasting. Someone battered him in Blue Town once. Makes you wonder what brought that on. But whatever it was, a dark cloud hung over our lives.

After junior school I attended Sheppey Comprehensive, later known as Minster

College. I really enjoyed drama, although part of me wishes I didn't because SD enjoyed it too. Even little connections, tiny similarities like that, make me sick.

Still into theatre, I enjoy going up to the West End to see musicals when I get the chance. I like all that type of music, but I judge myself for it. I tell myself it's not manly. Strangely, however, if I had a son, I would encourage him to listen to whatever music makes him happy. But I don't seem able to give myself that permission. It's a battle.

As I got into my teenage years, I became increasingly aware of gossip about SD. People always seemed to be talking about him. The more I heard, the more I understood. The local paper reported SD's transgressions. It was a struggle to contain my emotions. I became very uneasy, worrying that people were reading about him and connecting him to me. I grew paranoid. I used to cry at the school gates, because I was so intensely anxious.

But once I was in school, and with my friends – who never judged me – I was fine. I used to stay behind and take part in various activities, joining different clubs, so that I didn't have to walk out at the same time as everyone else. I was frightened I'd get beaten up but amazingly no one ever did say, or do, anything, but I became quite paranoid and if I saw a group of people giggling. I'd think it was me they were laughing at.

Once while waiting to go in to class I got a tap on the shoulder. Turning, I saw some lads laughing. They were probably just doing it to be annoying and it most likely wasn't personal, but I felt they were after me. I stopped going out. I went only to the youth club where I knew I was safe with my friends. I wouldn't go down town on my own, I wouldn't walk anywhere on my own. I became a recluse. I wanted to wear an invisibility cloak. I kept myself to myself and tried not to cause trouble.

Much later, when all my friends started going out drinking and clubbing, I used to stay at home. If we were going to play football I would go out with my good friends, but if there was a party or a social gathering where there'd be loads of people I didn't know, I wouldn't go. I had a constant knot in my stomach and just didn't feel safe. That feeling remains. Even now if I'm standing in a pub and just glancing around, as you do, if someone looks back at me, I think Shit, he's spotted me. I drink my beer and tell myself, Shit. Calm down, calm down. But then I want my friends to move pubs.

So in every possible way, I tried to stay under the radar. Unlike SD, of course. He had been plastered all over the local papers for being a Peeping Tom and stealing from the Christmas Lights' fund as well as the local carnival.

He always wanted to be seen as someone who was helping the community, so he'd get involved by playing Father Christmas and other things. Coming up to my GCSEs was the worst time. He was playing Santa up in Woking, Surrey – 70 miles away. He had to travel to play

Father Christmas because locally everyone knew him. But you can't run from bad headlines. The Sheerness Times Guardian had reported his various crimes and the story was picked up by the tabloids that this criminal was playing Santa. They papers published a picture of him as Father Christmas and printed his name and address.

I felt sick for days. One of the worst parts of it was that he was putting on this front of being a pillar of the community, but the truth was he hated Christmas. He'd go to midnight mass on Christmas Eve, so he said. But then he wouldn't want to get up on Christmas morning. Kev and I would be desperate to open our presents, but Mum made us wait until SD woke up in case he shouted at her for leaving him out of "the fun". By the time he got up, he was vile-tempered and we would wish he'd stayed in bed anyway. I don't remember Christmases when I was little. I don't remember opening toys or presents or eating dinner. I must have blocked them out. The only thing I remember is SD waking me up once while dressed as Father Christmas and scaring the crap out of me. For him to be playing Santa to other children was a sick joke.

Mum, Kev and I were afraid, paranoid, embarrassed and deeply ashamed. By contrast, SD walked about with his head held high, literally, He walked about as if he owned the island, like his shit didn't stink. It was us three who kept our heads down, who hid in doorways so he wouldn't see us. We were the ones carrying the shame and the fear of being attacked for someone else's crimes. He didn't care, and he had no shame, either, going so far even as to join a church; just another cover.

CHAPTER 5

"ARE you on drugs?" she asked.

I opened one eye and looked at the counsellor, tried to focus on the question.

"Ryan? Are you on drugs?"

I sat up as straight as I could. "What are you on about? I'm just knackered. All I want to do is sleep."

I was always in and out of counselling. I started going when I was 13, for anxiety. Kevin went too. Even in the sixth form, he was still playing with his Lego and very young children's toys such as My Little Pony and Sylvanian Families. I didn't think anything of it; I was used to him. But I realise now that he was trying to create little worlds to escape into because his own reality was too hard to deal with. He was also hanging around with girls at school and had good female friends, and he would later reveal to us that he was gay.

So I don't know if the counselling helped

him, but however, Mum organized it through her GP and took us both to Chatham. I would end up screaming in fear at the thought of going. Mum was trying to fix us but she didn't have the full picture – of my illness, and Kev's abuse. No one knew. On the occasion the therapist asked me if I was on drugs, I was emotionally drained and the truth was that I felt so safe in that room, I just kept dozing off. It was as if I could finally rest. I felt bad for doing it, but I couldn't help myself. I have read more about this recently and it could have been a shut-down response, basically playing dead, which the oldest part of our brain, our so-called "reptilian brain" does when we feel as if we are under threat. Most likely I was depressed, which can leave you feeling exhausted.

With the various counsellors, I would have a certain amount of sessions and then be discharged. Basically, you just talk it out until you feel a bit better and then you bugger off. You're meant to go back into society and feel completely healed but it was not like that for me. How could it have been?

I would cope for a bit but quickly go downhill and return for another 10-12 weeks of counselling. It was nearly always with a different therapist, so I'd have to start all over again, not continue where I left off. It was utterly pointless and a waste of resources. The NHS could save money long-term by giving you substantial counselling in the first place, but they don't. It's always this sticking plaster approach, patching you up and sending you back out into the world until you break again. It's a vicious circle. I liken it to giving someone with Type 1 Diabetes just enough insulin for a month. From the age of 13 to now, the counselling has been almost constant but with six-to-12-month breaks. I've seen about 20 different counsellors and psychiatrists of all kinds.

I carried on into sixth form at school, studying art as one subject, and applied to the Kent Institute of Art and Design (KIAD) at Rochester but I didn't get in. I did another year of sixth form to improve my grades before going to Swale Training Centre in Sittingbourne where I studied computer and graphic design. I really enjoyed that. I learned package design, and applied for a job in Covent Garden with the publisher, Dorling Kindersley. I got through the first stage but I never heard after that, and I was quite pissed off. But in reality, I don't think I would have coped with commuting to London.

Alongside my studies, I worked at Tesco, and just before I finished at Swale Training, an agency offered me a fruit packing job, which I did for a while before joining logistics company, GB Terminals. I worked there for 21 years but this year, in 2019, I took voluntary redundancy so that I can hopefully make a positive change in my professional life and maybe find something more stimulating and creative.

I miss my art. Occasionally, I draw – well, I doodle really. I haven't put pencil to paper properly for years. When I do draw – and it's rarely – I enjoy it. But it's that motivation to actually get going that's missing; I lack the self-belief. At school I used pencil and chalk. I enjoyed blending the colours. At Swale Training I had a considerable portfolio, but when I left I forgot to take it but it had been stolen when I went back to retrieve it.

CHAPTER 6

SHOULD I have been able to stop what happened next? It's a question I have asked myself more times than I can count. Should I be able to remember exactly when my father sexually assaulted me? That's another question I have asked myself. Other people have asked me too, implying that if I can't remember the exact date then it can't have happened. I know I was aged between 16 and 19.

"If you were 19, why didn't you stop him?"

That's the next question. But it doesn't work like that. I was still the frightened and controlled child mentally, no matter what age I was physically. I just want to scream at people that if they have questions then they should go and ask the perpetrator, the paedophile, the criminal in question. Don't ask the victim because guess what? It's not their fucking fault. Ask them how they are, what you can do to support them, but if you can't do that, fuck off.

I know why people ask these questions. Some people ask them because they're arseholes and they don't believe me. Other people ask because they think I'm dramatic and must be exaggerating. And of course, the main reason people ask is because it's such a horrifying thought. They are desperately trying to convince themselves that if it happened to them, their children or grandchildren, they could stop it happening; they wouldn't have become a victim; they would have stood up, fought back, kicked arse. Have you ever heard that Lady Gaga song Til It Happens to You? It's beautiful and in a subtle and articulate way, she attacks the doubters. If I'd written that song, it would have more along the lines of: "until it happens to you, offer me your belief, your sympathy and shut the fuck up about how it wouldn't have happened to you because you're wiser, stronger, better". It can happen to anyone. That's how crime works. That's how sexual abuse works. One minute it hasn't happened, then it's happening, then it's happened. It is wrong, it is completely traumatizing, and it breaks your world in two.

Do not, I repeat, do not blame the victim. And if you feel yourself opening your mouth to do that, shut it, go away and have a think about how you can be smarter than that. If you can't be smarter, stay the fuck away from the victim.

So I was aged somewhere between 16 and 19 and I'd had an argument with Mum, and after my shift at Tesco I went round to see SD. I was planning to stay the night. We were lying down watching TV and his hand moved and I just froze. Then he made me do things that I didn't want to do. I went along with it.

This isn't right, this is my Dad, I was thinking, the thoughts going round and round in my mind.

As I said, people think if they were assaulted or even raped that they'd fight back, do certain things. But until you're in that situation, you don't know what you would do. Most freeze, like an animal under attack, just wanting it to be over. That's what I did. The question should never be to the victim about why they did or did not do this or that; the responsibility lies with the criminal.

I'll repeat what I said earlier. The question should be asked of them, and only them: Why did you do that?

Afterwards, I left. I started to worry that I'd asked for it. I hadn't, of course. And even if I had, if I was gay, which I wasn't, I didn't want a sexual relationship with my own father. It wasn't consensual, it was a crime. He had a hold over me. I said nothing to anyone. I felt dirty. It should not have happened. It was confusing. It played on my mind, and still does.

I thought that if I carried on normally, no one would question anything. I went back, visiting SD again, although I was sure never to put myself into a vulnerable situation where it could happen again. It was the most abnormal thing that could have happened and my response was to act normal, which apparently is very common.

For those who want to know why abuse victims and survivors are sometimes hazy on the details, I think this from the Sidran Institute called "What Are Traumatic Memories?" explains it well:

> There is strong documentation to prove the high incidence of child abuse in the general population. Sexual abuse of children and adolescents is known to cause severe psychological and emotional consequences. Adults who were sexually abused in childhood are at higher risk for developing a variety of psychiatric disorders, including dissociative disorders (such as dissociative identity disorder/multiple personality disorder), anxiety disorders (panic attacks, etc.), personality disorders (borderline personality disorder, etc.), mood disorders (such as depression), PTSD, and addictions. In order to understand the essential issues about traumatic memory, one must first understand the human mind's response to a traumatic event.

> Psychological "trauma" is defined by the American Psychiatric Association as "an event or events that involved actual or threatened death or serious injury, or a threat to the physical integrity of self or others." Examples include military combat, violent personal attack, natural or human-made disasters, and torture. For children, sexually traumatic events may include age-inappropriate sexual experiences without violence or injury.

Like adults who experience trauma, children and adolescents who have been abused cope by using a variety of psychological mechanisms. One of the most effective ways people cope with overwhelming trauma is called "dissociation." Dissociation is a complex mental process during which there is a change in a person's consciousness which disturbs the normally connected functions of identity, memory, thoughts, feelings, and experiences (daydreaming during a boring lecture is a good example).

People may use their natural ability to dissociate to avoid conscious awareness of a traumatic experience while the trauma is occurring, and for an indefinite time following it. For some people, conscious thoughts and feelings, or "memories," about the overwhelming traumatic circumstance may emerge at a later date.

It is also common for traumatized people to make deliberate efforts to avoid thoughts or feelings about the traumatic event and to avoid activities or situations which may remind them of the event. In some severe cases, avoidance of reminders of the trauma may cause a person to have "dissociative amnesia," or memory blanks for important aspects of the trauma.

There are several factors that influence whether a traumatic experience is remembered or dissociated. The nature and frequency of the traumatic events and the age of the victim seem to be the most important. Single-event traumas (assault, rape, witnessing a murder, etc.) are more likely to be remembered, but repetitive traumas (repeated domestic violence or incest, political torture, prolonged front-line combat, etc.) often result in memory disturbance. The extremely stressful experiences caused by natural or accidental disasters (earthquakes, plane crashes, violent weather, etc.) are more likely to be remembered than traumatic events deliberately caused by humans (i.e. incest, torture, war crimes).

CHAPTER 7

AFTER SD sexually assaulted me, I got angrier and angrier. I had severe road rage and felt completely out of control, as if there was no justice in the world, that nothing was fair. This went on for seven or eight years into my early 20s. There was a hurricane building inside me. I slept around, trying to prove to myself that I wasn't gay, trying to have lots of sexual experiences to bury the one with SD, to push it as far back in history as possible. I drank a bit, tried a few drugs. Nothing worked.

A few years after the assault, SD came into some money and offered to take me to New York. I felt angry at him and thought that I would use him by going. It was a terrible mistake. We stayed in a hostel and every day he left me alone there for up to seven hours while he went off doing God knows what. But he eventually ran out of money, and I had to fund him using my credit card.

I gave him many chances but he never spent any quality time with me. He never treated me like a son, only like a possession or a showpiece to try and prove to himself, and others, that he was a man who could reproduce and play the good father.

After Kev finished sixth form, where he studied health and social care, he went to work at an old people's home called Oak Dean. He worked there for a couple of years and learned to drive at the same time. However, at the aged of 20, in 1993, Kev moved to London with a friend. He asked us to visit him and it was then he told us he was gay. He said he was so scared to come out because he thought we'd disown him. We knew, of course. It was something we always knew but didn't really think about or talk about. We just told him, "We still love you. As long as you're happy, we're happy," and he never looked back.

I went up and stayed with him in London. I'd train it into Victoria Station and we'd meet at WH Smith. We'd hang out for the weekend, chill, have some food and maybe go to the cinema. Kev was happy, relaxed and free and it was so nice to see. He had some nice boyfriends and a couple of not so nice ones, but he brought them all home to meet me and Mum.

Kev was comfortable up in London because it was a better scene for him, more accepting. He continued working in a care home, a job that he really liked. But there were stresses in his life, an unfounded complaint at work and then he and a friend witnessed a stabbing on a bus. Kev didn't want to go to court as a witness, but his mate put his name down and my brother was really worried about it. He lost a hell of a lot of weight; he almost looked anorexic, which was a big change as he had previously been very overweight. But he never lost touch with us and spoke often to Mum. Because he'd not been one to go out much while we were growing up, he'd become particularly close to our mother – and that didn't change.

CHAPTER 8

I MET my wife in 2003, and we fell in love.

I thought if I could change my life and get married and have kids, it would erase everything that had happened. I believed that if I could force myself to be happy in any way, shape or form, I would be able to quell the turmoil inside me.

My fiancée knew I wasn't functioning at 100 per cent, that I was depressed, got angry easily and panicked over making decisions. It could have been my illness, the abuse or my childhood with SD, I'll never know what caused what. And, of course, everything was linked because EID can be triggered by childhood trauma.

I kept the abuse a complete secret until I was due to be married. I had hinted at things but never been clear. It was just bubbling away beneath the surface.

One day, however, I thought, Enough is enough. I've got to say something if I'm going to spend the rest of my life with this woman.

I was perched on the side of the bed and it all came tumbling out. It wasn't easy but I did feel some relief. I was in and out of counselling at the time, and revealing the abuse made me see that maybe there was a reason why I was behaving the way I was.

My fiancée was great. She sat and listened, and she encouraged me to tell Mum. I felt shit scared; I thought she'd disown me or say I was making it up, despite the fact she hated SD for all the terrible things he had had done to her. I can't remember if I told Mum or if my fiancée did, but I do remember telling Kev on the phone.

"Ryan," he said. "It happened to me as well."

I couldn't believe what I was hearing. Kev had been abused by SD from the age of five.

"I thought that if I let him do it to me, then he wouldn't do it to you," he told me.

I think I felt angrier about Kev being abused than about my own experience. That might sound weird, but it was as if I let my brother down because he tried to protect me – but it still happened. Kev had put himself through all of that to protect me and it hadn't worked. I was raging because he had sacrificed himself to no avail. The sorrow I feel about that is overwhelming at times. I thought that speaking out about the abuse was going to make me feel better, but because I found out about Kev being abused, I felt worse. I felt even more anger towards SD for what my brother went through. That haunted me for ages and ages. My heart aches to think of it. Mum, naturally, was distraught. We tried to reassure her, but of course she blamed herself.

Not long after this, SD texted me to remind me of an important day coming up. He was referring to his mum's birthday, but I thought he meant Father's Day. I was furious, and my fiancée encouraged me to tell him what I thought. I texted him and said, "I don't care. I haven't got a Dad anymore. You're just a nasty piece of shit. Why celebrate Father's Day? I don't want anything to do with you."

We didn't do anything else. I wish we had gone to the police there and then. My life is full of ifs and buts. A few weeks later, my fiancée and I were pulling into a supermarket car park and we saw SD. She stormed out of the car and confronted him. I was terrified, but I followed her just in time to hear him say, "I never did anything to Kev. I never touched him. But Ryan asked for it." He turned to me and said, "Ryan, tell her you asked for it. You wanted it."

I froze. I was too shocked to speak. SD walked away with my fiancée shouting after him. We went back to the car and my mind was a whirl.

"I asked for it?" I said. "Can you believe that? He admitted it but blamed me?"

That really messed with my head for a long time. I started to wonder if I had given him some signal, whether I'd accidentally brushed against him. It's ludicrous how much it played on my mind. There's no way I had come onto my father, but even if I had, the correct response from him would have been: "Hold on, son, you've got some issues here. Do you think you're gay? What are you after? Because whatever you're after I'm not going to give you because I'm your father."

Whenever I was near him, I was that little boy. I know my sexuality now. I'm heterosexual and I don't fancy men. But for a long time, it did make me question a lot of things. Nobody understands it unless they go through it. But it makes you feel so dirty. It fucked me up and I was fucked up to start with.

On June 4, 2004, SD sent me a letter.

> Dear Ryan,
>
> You can imagine how I felt when you dropped your bombshell earlier this week. Whatever rights you think you may have, the way you did it was out of order. However, I am positive one or two others were behind this.
>
> I think it only fair to inform you that I have decided to seek legal advice over the matter, and have made an appointment to see my solicitor in the next two weeks. I have done this for two very good reasons, the first being I am not sure whether you have informed the police, and I can expect a visit from them at any time. The second is that it appears you have not been completely honest with yourself, I won't dwell on this at this moment in time, but I think you know

what I mean.

I think it would be in both our interests if you and I had a face to face meeting as soon as possible, strictly on our own of course without others listening. You can choose the time and place, but I would prefer in a public place. I can promise you as far as I am concerned it will be a cordial meeting. If you are in agreement to meet me then there is every chance I will call off my appointment with my solicitor. If I do not receive a positive response from you within the next few days I will exercise my rights, and keep my appointment, but I cannot promise that the outcome will be favourable for either of us.

I must say that the text comments from your girlfriend were completely over the top. I am sure that you have only told her what you wanted her to hear. If I had been completely honest with your Mother when I first met her things would have been a lot different now.

Finally, please don't take it out on your Nan, putting down the phone when she was talking to you was very bad manners. You must realise that if all that has happened these last few days gets back to her it could kill her. Do you really want that?

Dad.

I shat myself. I knew I hadn't done anything wrong, but I still thought he could get me into trouble. He was using scare tactics, and they worked. I never replied.

Reading between the lines now I can see he was scared that I was going to go to the police. Clearly he wanted to intimidate me with mentions of solicitors and how that wouldn't have a favourable outcome for either of us. He questioned my memory of events, a technique used by narcissists to control and weaken others, known as gaslighting. He wanted us to meet alone so that he could attempt to frighten me into silence. He used the death of my Nan as a threat. Psychologically the letter is coercive, abusive and manipulative. It's vile and it tells you everything you need to know about what a monster he was. Basically, he was admitting it but blaming me.

Ryan and his brother Kevin were always close.
Kevin sadly died of an aneurysm, aged 33, on June 25, 2007

CHAPTER 9

I TRIED to suppress everything that happened and carried on. We had a wonderful wedding in Jamaica and in 2004, our daughter was born. I was overjoyed and felt that my life had been given an infusion of happiness. I had someone else to think about. I was happy for Mum, who was delighted with her first grandchild and Kev who was thrilled to have a niece. The positives outweighed the negatives, for as long as they could.

But I still had my anxieties.

I would put the baby in her pram and push her through the high street, and for all the pride it brought me, if anyone looked in my direction I would imagine they were thinking I was going to abuse her.

Eventually I left the pram pushing to my wife because the paranoia had become too much. Later I would walk with my girls, holding their hands, but when they were first born I was frightened. I still worry about what people say about me but that's why I'm writing this book: to be honest and explain why I am the way I am.

Later that year, Kev dropped a bombshell. He was HIV positive. I was distraught, convinced this illness was going to shorten Kev's life. It didn't make sense to Mum. Like all parents, she thought she would go first and I think she blocked it out. But Kev kept telling us that new drugs were being developed all the time and that he was going to be okay. We took a lot of comfort from him and how positive he was being. Maybe I was being naïve. That said, I did worry about Kev infecting the baby. Like a lot of people at the time, and possibly even now, I didn't understand completely and was worried that Uncle Kev wouldn't be able to hold and kiss his niece. I knew he was gay and wouldn't have any kids of his own, so I wanted him to have a close relationship with his niece. I spoke to him and read the leaflets, so I could learn how the virus is transferred. Knowing the truth, I stopped worrying.

Despite his diagnosis, Kev seemed really happy. He left care work and started working with people with mental illness at Ealing Hospital in West London. Maybe he was sicker than he let on. After all, most of the time we spoke to him was on the phone when he could have been putting on a brave face. But apart from losing a huge amount of weight, he seemed okay.

Then one Friday evening, I called Kev and he said he was going to Manchester to meet a friend. The next day at work, I got a call from my wife saying there was a voicemail on the landline. It was Kev and he sounded weird. She played it down the phone to me and I could hear my brother saying, "Ryan please help me, I don't know where I am, I'm lost, I'm scared, help me, help me."

Because I was at work, my wife rang Kev – and Greater Manchester Police answered.

They had Kev at the police station. A milkman had found him wandering in the street, badly beaten. I went home and called the police back and told them I was on my way. I'd never driven that far before, but I borrowed a mate's SatNav to make sure I didn't get lost. All the way there, Kev kept ringing saying, "Are you coming to pick me up?"

"Yes," I was telling him.

"You're not lying to me, are you?"

"No, Kev, I'm coming."

He kept ringing Mum too, to check I was on my way. It was weird. I didn't know what the hell had happened, but he sounded panic-stricken.

I remember the moment when I completely changed as a brother. My wife and I pulled onto the forecourt of the police station and I looked over at what I assumed to be an old man sitting on the steps.

But it was Kevin.

He was in such a state; bruised, battered and almost lifeless. From that moment I was no longer the little brother. I was the big brother and Kevin needed my protection. I had to step up and become the protector.

I'm not letting anything else bad happen to you Kevin, I told myself.

I ran towards Kev and he leaped into my arms and held me tight. I asked him what had happened, but he refused to say so I went inside the station to have a chat with the police.

They said Kev had come to Manchester because he'd met someone online, but he'd been drugged and raped by two or three men. After the attack, he had drifted in and out of consciousness but eventually managed to find the front door of the house where he was held, and escape.

Kev never gave the police any of the details of the men who attacked him but while he was being interviewed, he mentioned SD's abuse and that over the years he had used cocaine and various other drugs, including alcohol, to numb the emotional pain. The drug use was a shocking revelation. I was horrified and upset.

One of the policewomen took my wife and me into another room and explained that she had a duty to pass the details of SD's abuse to Kent Police, our local force. I felt partially relieved that the ball was now rolling, and there was nothing we could do to stop it. It had been taken out of our hands. But on the other hand, I thought, Shit, this is it. Here we go.

We put Kev in the car and he crouched down, hiding in the back seat until we were physically out of Manchester and on the motorway. I showed him pictures of my daughter to try and take his mind off the trauma and when he saw her with Mum he said, "That's my mummy. I want my mummy."

It absolutely broke my heart to hear my older brother speaking as if he were a seven-year-old child. It was as if he'd been away on a school trip for two weeks and missed his mum.

When we got home, he hugged and kissed Mum like his life depended on it.

CHAPTER 10

"WE'RE going after SD. For Kev, Mum. Enough is enough. After what he's been through, I need to do something, to be able to say to him, 'There you go, Kev, I've sorted that out for you'."

Mum nodded. I wasn't even thinking about what happened to me that time, I wanted justice for Kev. He hated the thought of the pursuing SD for his crimes while Big Nan was alive. "I can't do it to her, Ryan," he said.

"I'm sorry, mate," I said. "But it's been taken out of our hands. His time's up, we've got to nail the bastard."

The next day I had to take some rubbish to the tip. Kev came with me and while we were out Mum and my wife called our local police in Swale. Two officers came the next day. One of them, Jan Robey, would become an amazing ally to our family. The officers were aware of

SD and all his previous, but they didn't know he had two sons. They interviewed Kev and tried to reassure him that he would be doing the right thing if he made a statement.

Kev had developed Aids by that point, but he was on medication and was stable. A couple of days after the policewomen had visited, he woke up in the middle of the night screaming my name. He was in terrible pain and had been sick. I called an ambulance and he was diagnosed with gastroenteritis.

For the next couple of days, he was very subdued. On the Friday he had his weekly check-up at Chelsea and Westminster Hospital. He was adamant about going even though we said we should ring them and explain that he was unwell. We wanted him to stay home and rest. He made it to the appointment, however, but the stomach trouble wasn't abating so he was admitted to hospital. On the Friday, Mum stayed with him in London, returning to Sheppey on the Saturday. On the Sunday I rang the hospital to check-up on him just before I went to work. The nurses said Kev was keeping his food down and when I spoke to him, he said he was feeling better. It was a relief. But 15 minutes after we'd hung up our call, he was found collapsed, clinically dead, on the hospital floor. The hospital said they would keep him alive until we got there.

Kev's boyfriend came from Greenwich to collect Mum and me. As we drove, the hospital kept ringing us to see if were getting close. The situation was clearly critical.

When we arrived, we got the bad news. Kev had suffered an aneurysm. It had burst and made his brain swell so much that the swelling had spread to his spinal column. If he survived he would be in a vegetative state. We all broke down.

I rang his close friends who had worked with Kev and who we had heard him speak about a lot.

"Do you want to come over because I don't think it's going to be long," I told them.

Before long, my wife arrived. Soon enough, a group of us clustered around Kev's bed. We remained there all night, telling stories and talking about him, talking to him. He never responded, but despite the grim reality confronting us, laughter also filled that room as we reminisced.

The nurses kept coming and checking on him, lifting up his eyelids. I can picture that as clear as day, seeing his eyes staring back, all the life gone from them.

Tubes ran from his body. Machines beeped constantly. It was so traumatic for us all, especially Mum – her baby.

The machines, of course, kept him alive. We were eventually asked if we were ready to switch them off. It was the hardest of decisions – but also the easiest. Kev didn't need to suffer any more. It was time for the last goodbye.

I gave him a kiss and a cuddle and said, "I'm sorry about the arguments we had when we were younger. Sleep well."

We left the room so the nurses could remove

the machinery. On our return, we stood as the colour drained out of him. He was no more. It was a relief in some respects that he had no more pain. His body had been hurting; it had been agonizing to watch. My big brother who had become so small, my protector who I had wanted to protect, my playmate and my buddy, was gone.

CHAPTER 11

"FUCK," I said. "Getting SD done isn't going to happen now is it? Kev never made his statement." I was driving home from hospital and had called Jan Robey. "He's got away with it again."

Jan was deeply sorry to hear about Kev and you could hear the disappointment regarding SD in her voice too.

"We can use what Kevin said as a character reference," she said. "But it can't be used to prosecute him. It won't be sufficient."

I almost didn't grieve at first because I was concentrating on what was going to happen to SD. I helped Mum organise the funeral but pure rage was bubbling inside me. I wanted SD done for murder as well as sexual abuse because I felt that everything he had done to Kev had pushed my brother into the life choices he had made, the drugs, and meeting up with random men. I wanted to scream in SD's face that he had murdered my brother, but I didn't want him to know that Kev had died as he would have come to the funeral and made it all about him. For that reason, I decided not to tell Big Nan. It was heartbreaking but I had no choice. We told people to keep the details to themselves. I think if he had have turned up there would have been a queue of people wanting to stab him. I wanted to kill him myself but then he would have been the victim and I would have been the perpetrator – and he would have loved that too much.

We decided not to wear black at the funeral. I wore a pink shirt with a pink tie. We found it hard to choose songs but there was one we definitely wanted to walk out of the crematorium to, which was Dancing Queen by Abba.

We were a bit concerned about the finances. Kev had no money but the funeral director let us set up a payment plan and we pulled in a favour from the vicar. I couldn't read anything even though I wanted to. I wished I'd ask to be a pall bearer so I could have carried my brother in, but I know I had to be by Mum's side the whole time. There was no way I was leaving her.

Kev often told me he didn't have any friends, but the church was packed. People were standing up the back because they couldn't get a seat. It was lovely to see.

Many came from his job at Ealing Hospital,

and a couple of weeks later, Mum, my wife, Kev's boyfriend and I went there for a memorial service. The patients' band played and a slide show of images depicting Kev's work with the patients was screened. It was really nice

After the funeral and the memorial service I couldn't relax properly because I knew that I had to carry on seeking justice for Kev. I didn't want his life to be in vain.

CHAPTER 12

THE day finally came. SD was arrested.

That was the day he was also told of Kev's death.

He was arrested at Big Nan's house and gave his mother his usual line – just helping the police with their enquiries.

After the arrest, the care home where Nan occasionally went for respite came to collect her so I went to visit so I could let her know about Kev and SD.

She blamed herself for Kev's death. She was convinced that she'd caused the aneurysm by kissing him on the head the last time she had seen him. Naturally I told her not to be so daft, but she was distraught.

I then told her the truth about SD. When I explained what he had done to Kev, she said nothing. But you could see in her eyes that she knew; she just didn't want to admit it.

I wasn't angry with her. She was sticking up for her son. Most parents would have done the same.

While being interviewed by police, SD revealed that his father had abused him. I felt so sick. I thought, There's no way my grandad could've done it. But who knows? Even so, I found it appalling that he had used that as an excuse. Why would you want to do it to someone else? It happened to me but there is no way I would do anything to my girls.

The police charged SD with sexual contact with minors. He was bailed and went directly to the office of the Sheerness Times Guardian to place an announcement about Kev's death. I felt sick when I saw it, all these gushing words about his son and how devastated he was. Maybe he knew the police would tell the paper about the charge and thought the reporters might go easy on him if they thought he was recently bereaved. It was typical of him though; making it all about himself, begging for sympathy.

SD appeared initially at Sittingbourne Magistrates Court before the case was sent to Crown Curt in Maidstone. I was shit scared about standing up in court in front of SD, absolutely terrified. Jan Robey very kindly organized a tour round the court a few weeks beforehand so that I would feel more comfortable. There I was, in my 30s, being guided around the court because of the state they thought I'd be in.

Sometime after I did the tour, SD was taken to hospital. They called me as I was his next of kin. He had a brain tumour apparently, but neither Mum nor I believed it as he was always crying wolf, saying he'd got various cancers over the years. But this turned out to be the real deal; he had 24 hours to live.

I didn't want to see him at first, but then I thought, If I don't go I'm not going to get an opportunity in court to stand up and tell him what he'd done and what I felt.

It was a good opportunity to speak and not have him interrupt me. He wouldn't be able to worm himself out of it. I was in control.

I visited him at Medway Maritime Hospital. I had to steel myself, but there were things he needed to hear.

When I came to his bedside, I bent down and whispered in his ear.

"I can't believe you're going to get away with this. I hope you rot in hell."

I would have liked to have screamed at him, maybe even grabbed a weapon and carved him up. If I could have got away it, I could have put a pillow over his head or something like that but then I would have had that on my conscience.

As far as I know, he died alone.

I had planned to attend his funeral, only to accompany Big Nan. But on the day I had to tell her I just couldn't bring myself to go. I would have felt like a hypocrite. My wife and I went to the Dickens World theme park in Rochester instead.

After the funeral, however, my uncle rang me.

"It's lucky you didn't go," he said.

"Why?"

"There were so many people there from his church saying how much of a shame it was and how he was such a lovely person. They couldn't believe he wasn't told about Kevin's death and wanted to know why his youngest hadn't been there."

"Isn't it incredible how stupid people are," I said to my uncle. "I can't believe how many people he fooled."

With SD dead, part of me was relieved I didn't have to stand up in court and be cross-examined by his defence team. I don't know how I would've reacted; the fear of it had been paralysing. Mum said that Kev didn't want me to go through it and had taken SD. But I was willing to push through my anxiety to see justice being done. I would've done anything for Kev at that point in life. I know that if SD had gone to court and got away with it, I would have wanted to kill him. I might even have done it although I hope not: I'm not that person. But who knows what I would have been capable of? Mum says I need to let it go and I sometimes think that I have. She feels that she never married SD, that she just had two beautiful boys who are nothing to do with him. She has blocked it out to survive.

When it was all over, I was numb, absolutely numb. It was all too much; I couldn't process any of it – the attack of Kev in Manchester, his death, going to the police, SD's arrest, the charges, preparing to go to court, and finally his death.

Did we get justice in the end? Yes, because SD died. But I wanted him in prison getting beaten up by other inmates. I wanted him to feel fear and pain, and to suffer like he made Kev suffer all those years. I wanted Kev to play with Lego and My Little Pony and be happy because he wanted to play with those toys; not because they were a means for him to escape his anguish.

I can still picture clearly a day when I was at work a few weeks after Kevin passed away. The sun shone. I closed my eyes for a few seconds. A vision of Kevin floated towards me. He put his arms around me. I felt a deep warmth envelop me for a few wonderful seconds. It was the best and most comforting feeling I've ever had. If I try, I can still feel it.

CHAPTER 13

I HOPED that by telling my wife about the abuse it would help me. But then I was floored by the devastating fact that Kev had been abused and had kept quiet in an attempt to protect me. That broke me. Then, before I knew it, Kev was sick and dying, the court case loomed, SD died, and it was over – but not in the way that I wanted.

My first daughter was young. We hadn't had our second yet. My life had shattered into countless pieces and through it all I was trying to be a husband and a father. It wasn't possible. My wife and I weren't getting along. Our relationship was not in a good place and I had an affair. I don't excuse that in any way, and I'm still paying for it now. Even though my wife was often hugely supportive, I question whether my marriage came at the right time and was with the right person. But I absolutely do not regret having our children.

We broke up in 2009 when our youngest was a year old. It would have been quite incredible if our marriage had been able to withstand all the slings and arrows, I suppose.

I overdosed, had my stomach pumped, was discharged and given a phone number to call to go back to counselling. I felt disappointed in myself, and stupid. But the way I was treated – as if I were a nuisance – made it a hundred times worse.

I hopped from relationship to relationship after my marriage ended. I've got a reputation, I know I have. I am scared to be alone. If I'm alone, I think too much. Being with someone is a distraction. I am actually looking for stability but that can be bad because I'll stay in unhealthy relationships. It's not good. I know that. If I see problems brewing in a relationship, I won't break it off because I don't want to hurt the other person. So I go about it the wrong way. I look for another relationship often before ending the one I should be dealing with. Then, of course, I get dumped and the abandonment I feel because of that, is sometimes more than I can bear. I know all this about myself; I recognise all my faults. Sometimes wonder if it would be easier to have no self-awareness and just be a bastard. It can be worse to know you have a flaw and to struggle to change that about yourself than not to know at all, I think. But what can I do? I am working on being better.

After SD died, I was confused and

emotionally all over the place. I hated him so much but at the same time, I was full of grief for the father I had never had. I was relieved that he couldn't hurt anyone else but angry that he had got away with everything. I felt guilty that he died alone but I was also happy that he had. I cried when I got the news that he'd finally gone but I kicked myself for being distraught. I was upset for everything he had taken from me, including my brother. My mind was all over the place.

I had always been anxious and explosive and it got worse. I was really suffering, having huge angry outbursts. I didn't know that I was ill. I just thought I'd had a shit life and it had made me that way. I would make mountains out of molehills. I would bottle up what had happened during the day and take it out on those closest to me. But as the years passed, and it got worse, I would shout at anyone.

From 2012 to 2016 I was in a long-term relationship. During this time, I tried to kill myself again by walking into the sea, but my partner found me in time. On another occasion, I left a note for her, one for Mum and one for my girls. I went for a drive and ended up at my counsellor's office. He made a call to the crisis team, which gives urgent help to mental health patients, and they finally got to me at 3am the following morning. They visited me every day for a week and sent me back to the Medway Memorial Hospital.

There, I received a diagnosis:

"It sounds like you've got Borderline

Personality Disorder, or Emotional Intensity Disorder as it's called now."

"What's the hell's that?"

That was it. A tiny explanation. No offer of any treatment or follow-up. I was on my own. I sat in the car park outside and Googled the symptoms. It's the worst thing to do really, but I had to try and understand until I got the help I needed. I looked down the list of symptoms. It was me. It was as if someone had switched a light on, but the light was black. I had more anxiety than ever. Everything made sense but it made me feel completely hopeless.

I finally understand who I am but THIS is who I am? Shit.

I had always been physical with my anger, punching doors and pillows. But after the diagnosis, I started punching myself in the chest. It was massive release, which is the point of self-harming, to make internal feelings external, to get them out of yourself. But it's dangerous and deeply disturbing to those around you. Once I asked a colleague to punch me in the face. It sounds ridiculous but I needed it and I couldn't see why he'd found it so disturbing. My bosses weren't impressed and work, which was already difficult due to my meltdowns and time off, became even worse. One of the symptoms of EID is doing and saying inappropriate things at inappropriate times. I am compulsive and impulsive. I know that. And no one understands. How could they? I didn't even understand myself. Others were being cut some slack for various issues and illnesses, but never me. I was expected, as are so many people with mental illness, to pull myself together. Do people not think that if I could, I would?

I was in a bad way, feeling more depressed and desperate than ever. The punching of doors and self-harming continued and one day I hit myself in the forehead. The feeling was intense and incredible. I realized I was able to get the negative feelings that were inside of me out so much quicker. Hitting myself in the chest was no longer enough. I was so furious to have the illness and I wanted to punish myself. I would stand at work and think constantly about throwing myself in front of the next truck that came along, or climbing the light tower that illuminates the yard at night. I could be falling from there and it could be over in a few seconds, I would tell myself. No one's going to stop me.

Thank goodness I never did it. I do have a lot to live for, mainly my girls. I've promised myself that I will be there for them no matter what but at the time, the feeling of complete despair and self-hatred was overwhelming.

As always, Mum was beside me every step of the way. She never failed me. I had periods of counselling and then, when I'd lost my shit again, Mum called the mental health team at Medway Memorial Hospital in tears.

Finally I was referred to the STEPPS program for those with EID. No one had ever suggested that to me before. How come? I hadn't even been told that such a thing existed, that there was any kind of help. The course was full up and I was told I'd go on a waiting list. When we didn't hear anything, which would be for months at a time, we called again. To say it was frustrating is an understatement. You don't have to chase hospitals for chemotherapy, worrying that they've forgotten you, do you? And here I was, trying to live with a broken mind, and begging for the help I needed to survive.

CHAPTER 14

I JOINED the STEPPS program in December 2016. The first thing we did was to look at our filters, the ways in which EID makes us view the world. The hardest part is looking into yourself more than you've ever done before. You're not picking yourself apart but you are separating yourself into different sections each time you attend. It's mind-blowing what you learn about yourself. And exhausting.

But the most amazing part of the course was meeting other people with the same illness. Before, I thought I was the only one. I didn't know anyone else with the condition because nobody ever spoke about it. I could've cried when I realised I wasn't alone. I think I probably talked and shared too much through sheer relief!

It was wonderful to have somewhere where I could be me, 100 per cent, where if I'm having a bad day I can be accepted. I can sit there and be quiet, or cry, scream or shout and I'm will not be judged. If I wanted to walk out of the group and take five minutes out, I could do that without guilt. The freedom was a magical feeling.

*

Failure to achieve is the big filter for me, the strongest. I feel that 90 per cent of that is not having a role model. I've said this to friends many times, but I would love to be a proper, stereotypical man who can build and fix things; simple stuff like DIY and cooking. I don't bother trying because I know I'm going to fail. Even thinking about it gets me stressed. So where cooking's concerned, for example, I bung in a microwave meal.

Thinking about DIY causes me to experience very intense emotions. I feel angry that SD wasn't a normal father who taught me things, like how to put up a shelf. We never bonded over such practical things. Not being able to do these things bothers me because I feel that these are what normal people do. I should be able to stand on my own two feet instead of relying on other people. My mates do all their own DIY but there's something inside me where I just don't get it. I think that every man should be a masculine man who can do DIY like old-fashioned men. I'm not saying that I am old fashioned and want dinner on the table when I get home, but I wish I could help out more with cooking and doing the DIY around the house like a modern man should be. I just beat myself up about it. I would have loved it if I'd had the type of father that had taught me to fish. Something as simple as that. All the blokes I worked with at GB went fishing at the weekends. So with SD, I have this dismissive name for him and I don't care, but I also wish he'd been different.

I feel like half the time I'm not a man's man. I'm the only bloke I know who cries. I've now turned this round to: "Okay, SD didn't show me how to do anything useful but he did show me how not to be; how not to be a father. As long as I never do anything he' did, I'll be better man than he ever was."

Sometimes I think should I change my surname from Harland so I am not burdened by that association with SD. But why should I? I have had too many years of hiding and keeping my head down so no one spots the connection between us. Now I want to be proud of who I am, despite having him as a father.

My entitlement filter told me that the world owed me everything. But now I realise I'm not entitled to be saved, I have to do that for myself. Entitlement is a hard one because we all deserve things and if you have low self-esteem, which abuse survivors and those with mental illness often have, you feel you are entitled to nothing.

I never got excited about holidays with my ex-partner because I thought, I don't deserve this. Why am I going away to nice places I don't deserve? A person like me going there… no way.

But you don't want to go the other way and think that you're owed everything. It's a balancing act. You have to do the work, even though it is knackering. But it's worth it and worth waking up every day and making the future better. Entitlement can work positively and negatively. It's the way you analyse it. "I'm entitled to have a nice future" doesn't mean "I'm going to sit back and everyone is going to make my future nice for me"; it's that I'm entitled to work my arse off and earn these things.

Part of my condition is that I accept the negative and brush away – or gloss over – the positives. I still do it now. I could put something up on Facebook and have loads of lovely comments, but if I get a negative one I will focus on that and forget all the affirmative ones. It just weighs on me, pushes me down and makes me more miserable. Then, when I am having a good time and I know I am, I feel good. But for whatever reason, I start feeling negative because I'm waiting for something to happen. Being this way ruins the nice time even before anything bad has happened, or will happen. It turns things into a negative, and for some reason I just feel more comfortable in that situation, even though I hate it and I wish things weren't like that. Without realising it, nine times out of 10, I turn things negative because that's what I know. When things are going well, I don't know how to embrace those moments, go with them and enjoy them. That's because there's been more negatives than positives. I feel more comfortable in the negative and know how to deal with it since I've been there so many times before.

I feel guilty about everything. I think that everything is my fault; that so many things wouldn't have happened if I didn't have this illness. If someone doesn't reply immediately to a text, I assume I've upset them. If someone walks past me at work and they've got a face like thunder, I wonder what I've done to upset them.

*

Before the course I had no idea what filters were. Now I feel that I have some understanding and I hope that I will be able to fit into society more. My anxiety has decreased to an extent because a lot of that was triggered by fear of every interaction setting off my filters and a range of feelings that I couldn't cope with, although I didn't know that this is what was happening.

Each week after our STEPPS session, we were given homework. I could see that the course was about understanding the illness, learning how the mind of someone with EID works (or doesn't!) and how I might be able to manage my problems better.

It helped me cope. For example, one week my girls' mobile phones were switched off and I couldn't speak to them. In the past I might have phoned my ex-wife and had a go at her. But during the course I learned that didn't get me anywhere. So I just texted the girls each day, told them I was worried and that I was looking forward to speaking to them, and waited. It breaks my heart when I can't speak to them, but over time they will realise that I am there for them. The best thing I can do for them is to focus on my health and try to stay well.

In many situations in life there are agendas and people playing games. I now try to refuse to become part of other people's agendas or to play the games they're playing.

I also try to acknowledge that me having this illness is really, really difficult for others. I can be intense, unpredictable and overwhelming. My illness and how it causes me to behave causes other people to experience anxiety, stress and emotional pain. There are two sides to this and I hope that people can get to a point where they can acknowledge their own pain that I may have contributed to and find ways to cope, but also acknowledge that I am living with a terrible illness. Feeling one does not have to cancel out the other. I will continue to try to be deeply compassionate towards myself and others. I hope they can do the same.

As I got into the course, I started to see that I can't change the past. I will never know whether the abuse caused or triggered my illness. The chances are it was always there, lurking. I do know that trauma and abuse haven't helped my illness and have undoubtedly made it worse.

But either way, STEPPS helped me break my illness down and make it more manageable. I now deal with things differently; not always, but as much of the time as possible. I try to be less impulsive, and get less frustrated.

If I'm in an argument, instead of immediately lashing out, I think: If I say that, will it cause more problems? Will this person really understand how I feel?

The answers to those questions are usually "Yes" and "No" respectively, so I don't engage because at that time everyone's emotions are too intense for me to get involved without adding to that intensity. I take myself off and do some breathing exercises or just sit and close my eyes.

I feel that I have people I can go to for support now who really understand how I feel. I belong to a support group on Facebook, which is a place for me to share my feelings instead of on my own page where – because my feelings can be so extreme – other people either don't know how to react, or what I'm saying brings up feelings for them that they haven't dealt with. So they either ignore me, accuse me of seeking attention or lash out and basically tell me to pull myself together.

Now, I can chat to people all over the world who have the same condition and get things off my chest without pissing anyone off. I have that freedom to express myself and not be judged.

And it doesn't always have to be extremely negative things. Recently I posted that although I feel like I'm a good place, I have this persistent sense that I'm not allowed to be happy. I wrote: "Everything in my life at the moment is going well but I can't help feeling down all the time and can't shake this negative feeling. I'm trying to stay positive but it's getting harder each day."

So many sympathetic comments poured in that even though I'm finding things difficult, knowing I'm not alone helps. And I enjoy being there to encourage others when I'm having a good day and they're not. I can be myself there. I don't need to ask permission to be ill when I'm interacting with the page. I'm not hurting anyone. It's a relief for me.

This course has helped me understand and make little changes in the way I deal with situations. Sometimes I feel like I'm the only one changing and everyone else is staying the same. Sometimes I do feel it's unfair and wonder why I've got to change to make other people accept me more while they make no changes.

But at the end of the day the course is for me and that's the reason I'm still doing it. When I have more of a handle on my illness, maybe I'll see who in my life is positive and who is negative, and I'll feel empowered to make some changes.

I've noticed that some people don't want me to get better, they want me to stay the same. But I'm not changing, really: I'm healing. Who wouldn't want me to heal? Change scares people. They try and knock me down a peg or two so I don't change so much in case they lose me. But they'll lose me anyway if they refuse to allow me to grow; that's just pushing me away.

Getting the diagnosis, researching the condition myself and going through STEPPS, a therapy specific to my illness, has been like slotting together an enormous jigsaw. For years there has been so much that I couldn't see or understand. I am now accepting that I am not a bad person. I am getting to know myself. I don't want to hurt people and to those that I have, I want to say sorry. I'm 41 and if I don't accept myself now, when will I? I accept, embrace and want to get as much control over this illness as possible.

I'm able to control myself better too. For example, when I was working at GB, I might be trying to explain something to my bosses about how a colleague's way of working made my job difficult. I might feel like they weren't listening and would storm off and chuck a chair, but now I'm aware that my reactions are down to my filters.

Most workers who try to speak to their bosses about something and don't get the response they want would either try again, go off and moan to a mate or partner, speak to someone in personnel or write an email. Those are all healthy, reasonable reactions that don't cause a scene and will potentially get the situation resolved.

For me, because of the way my brain works, I perceive that I am being ignored, I am unloved, the group has abandoned me and therefore I am vulnerable, will be sick forever and possibly die as a result. It reaffirms my sense that I can't trust anyone and that I am incapable of achieving anything. And all these feelings rush at me in a matter of seconds, an overwhelming wave of stuff I can't cope with – which is why I throw a chair; because at that moment I am in great pain. The course has helped me break down and understand that pain, and why my brain feels those things.

Not everyone at work was thrilled with me having the time off for STEPPS. Some people wanted me to be able to control myself because they need to believe that if they were mentally ill, they could control themselves. It's the same with sexual abuse, which people feel they could stop happening. Colleagues, therefore, would stop and ask me why I needed to leave work. But no one would ask that if I was having physio for surgery on my shoulder, would they?

I got to a point where, if I felt overwhelmed at work, I would try to behave differently. I would go for a walk, have a fag, deep breathe or just do a little dance. I try to switch off my mind to stressors by changing the subject, or playing a game on my phone.

I've developed tools to help me cope with my symptoms. I'm never going to be perfect. No one is perfect. We're all allowed to get angry, upset, pissed off, down, miserable, but now I know I've got the tools to cope with it more easily. I am quicker to calm myself down. I'm not sure how, it's been a drip-drip effect the things I've learned. I have a more positive attitude and outlook on life. I'm proud that I have now run the London Marathon three times, in 2017, 2018 and 2019 raising money for Whizz-Kids the first two years and for Get Kids

Going this year.

With SD, I'm at the point where can see that I shouldn't have dwelled on it for so long. I'll never forgive him. I can't change what happened. But I choose to look to the future instead of at the past.

Going through this process has made me very compassionate, and since I'd rather be a caring guy than a shit guy, I can honestly say that the illness has forged me into who I am, and I am grateful for it. I wouldn't change that.

CHAPTER 15

AFTER STEPPS comes Stairways. It's a similar program, treading over the same ground but in greater detail. We began with 18 of us on STEPPS, but those numbers dwindled to six, and finally three of us moved onto Stairways. It's a huge commitment and not everyone manages it.

It's so hard to know which parts of my mental suffering is due to my illness and which of it is the immense trauma I've suffered. Not just with SD – the abuse, the court case, him dying just before justice – but also Kev. It is a life-changing thing to lose a brother and to an illness which in itself is so unfair.

I've come to terms with what happened in the past and I've accepted it and it's made me the person I am today. I have a big heart; I don't judge anyone and I take them on face value. I help people as much as I can; if somebody has a problem I'm always the type of person to sit there and listen to them and give them the best advice that I can.

Maybe I've been dealt a shit hand and there have been times when I wanted to fold that hand, like in poker. But life's not a card game, so I can't. I've wanted to take my own life but I won't because I think I have a purpose: to tell my story and hopefully help other people. Is it destiny? I don't know. I believe that we are all put here for a reason and I feel like this book is my reason for being here. I've been wanting to write it for 10 years. But why was this path given to me?

I know there are people out there whose lives are a so much worse than mine; their paths have been terrible. But on the other hand, why do some people breeze through life? Why do some get handed a path that leads to fame and fortune, everything handed to them on a plate?

The other side of the coin is that it might all be random. It probably is. It's probably the choices we make through life that decide where we go. Perhaps myself, now, going through intense therapy for EID and writing this book is the T-junction in my life. And now I'm choosing to leave this path and choose another that is much better for me, and ultimately this is where I'm supposed to be – I am, at last, on the right path.

When I think back to my childhood, when Kevin and I wrote to Ladybird asking them to print our book, I could never have imagined that this would be the story that I would actually end up writing. I hope my brother is at peace now. I hope Mum has many happy and healthy years ahead of her. I hope SD rots in hell like I told him to.

And me? I'm holding out for a happy ending. Some peace in my heart and some joy in my life. I hope I get it.

EPILOGUE

I FEEL it is important to mention that I do have another brother. He was the result of a relationship SD had before he met Mum. We found out about him in the years leading up to Kev's death and they had a good relationship. I found the situation difficult to accept but I am glad to have a relationship with him now, and to have been invited to his wedding. He was adopted at birth and feels lucky that he escaped being brought up by SD. He had great, loving parents who gave him everything including a good education. I feel brotherly towards him. I don't treat him like he's replaced Kev because no-one can, but it's nice to know I have someone to go to for advice or to just offload. He's a genuine guy.

HELPFUL ORGANISATIONS

www.mind.org.uk
Call: 0300 123 3393 9am to 6pm daily
Email: info@mind.org.uk
Text: 86463

www.youngminds.org.uk
For parents who are concerned about a young
person's mental health.
Call: 0808 802 5544

www.childline.org.uk
For young people who need someone to talk to,
call 0800 1111

www.napac.org.uk
The National Association for People Abused in
Childhood. Call free: 0808 801 0331, Monday-
to-Thursday 10am-9pm and Friday 10am-6pm

www.mosac.org.uk
For mothers of sexually abused children
Call: 0800 980 1958

www.samaritans.org
Whatever you're going through, a Samaritan
will face it with you. We're here 24 hours a day,
365 days a year
Call: 116 123
Email: jo@samaritans.org

www.survivorsuk.org
For male survivors of rape and sexual abuse
Call: 0203 598 3898

www.pandasfoundation.org.uk
PANDAS Foundation vision is to support every
individual with pre (antenatal), postnatal
depression or postnatal psychosis in England,
Wales and Scotland.
Call: 0843 28 98 401 every day from 9am-8pm

www.switchboard.lgbt
Provides information, support and referral
services.
Call: 0300 330 0630 From 10am to 10pm daily
Email: chris@switchboard.lgbt (response in 72
hours)
Live chat available on the website

www.carersuk.org
Making life better for carers
Call: 020 7378 4999

ABOUT THE AUTHOR

Ryan Harland was born on the Isle of Sheppey, Kent, in 1977, and has lived on the island all his life. He was diagnosed with EID some seven years ago. He is the father of two daughters. Riding the Storm is his first book.

Made in the USA
Coppell, TX
07 July 2021

58664514R00059